To:

From:

FATHERS ARE SPECIAL

A TRIBUTE TO THOSE WHO ENCOURAGE, SUPPORT, & INSPIRE

COMPILED BY
LUCY MEAD

GRAMERCY BOOKS
NEW YORK

This 2000 edition is published by Gramercy™ Books , an imprint of Random House Value Publishing, Inc. 201 East 50th Street, New York, N.Y. 10022

Gramercy™ Books and design are trademarks of Random House Value Publishing, Inc.

Random House
New York • Toronto • London • Sydney • Auckland
http://www.randomhouse.com/

Interior Design: Karen Ocker Design, New York

Printed and bound in Singapore.

Library of Congress Cataloging–in–Publication Data

Fathers are special / compiled by Lucy Mead.
         p.   cm.
   ISBN 0-517-20956-X (hc.)
    1. Fathers Quotations, maxims, etc.   2. Fathers Anecdotes.
  3. Fathers Poetry.   I. Mead, Lucy.
  PN6084.F3F384 2000
  306.874'2--dc21
                                                           99-43265
                                                           CIP

Fathers are Special

My father taught me to work; he did not teach me to love it. I never did like to work, and I don't deny it. I'd rather read, tell stories, crack jokes, talk, laugh—anything but work.

ABRAHAM LINCOLN

My father said to me, "never do a job that can be replaced by machines." So I thought being an actor was a job that can't be replaced by machines. But it looks as though we might be getting to that stage.

MICHAEL CAINE

My father was often angry when I was most like him.

LILLIAN HELLMAN

I like being prepared. When things are going on and I have to learn my lines at the last minute, I'm never quite secure enough to allow it to be spontaneous...Yeah, look, I have a very strong work ethic, you know?...I've said it. It's from my dad. He really instilled that in all of us as children.

MICHELLE PFEIFFER

"How do you feel about your daughter dating? Are you good about that?"

"Well, we have a deal where they're not allowed to have sex until after I'm dead. So, so far it's been fine."

BILLY CRYSTAL

She got her good looks from
her father—he's a plastic surgeon.

GROUCHO MARX

Forget about the dough. Go in there and
show them what you can do. Make yourself
so valuable that they just gotta have you.

CLINT EASTWOOD SR. *to his son*

My father basically taught me, showed me how a man treats
a lady. I don't know if that's extraordinary or not. To me it's
standard. My father demanded a certain amount of respect,
and he gave it."

WHITNEY HOUSTON

From my dad I think I got a great sense of humor about life and sort of an ease with children that he had...he was very warm and loving, a very hands-on type of dad that you didn't really see in the '50s and '60s.

DENNIS QUAID

My father died when I was fifteen. So the advice I basically remember the most, he'd always say, "Be a man." Whatever that meant, I knew what that meant. It was, "Take it. Take it like a man." And it also had a lot to do with honesty and integrity because that was what he was all about. So that's the best advice I ever had a chance to get from him."

BILLY CRYSTAL

I would say we moved around quite a bit. Every time the rent came due, my father carried the furniture on his back to some new place. For thirty years, I thought we were in the furniture business.

JACKIE MASON

People used to think that my father
was like Willy Loman, but he was quite
the opposite. You know, writers
sometimes invent stuff.

ARTHUR MILLER

Are you lost daddy, I asked tenderly.
Shut up, he explained.

RING LARDNER

We think our Fathers Fools, so wise we grow;
Our wiser Sons, no doubt, will think us so.

ALEXANDER POPE

I cheat my boys every chance I get. I want to
make 'em sharp. I trade with the boys and skin 'em
and I just beat 'em every time I can.

WILLIAM A. ROCKEFELLER, *father of John D. Rockefeller*

As long as I have been in the White House, I can't help
waking at 5 A.M. and hearing the old man at the foot of the
stairs calling and telling me to get out and milk the cows.

HARRY S. TRUMAN

My father was devoted to his children, but sometimes he seemed even more devoted to our three dogs, Harley, Casey and Thatcher. They each had a special, fluffy, tartan wool bed to match their tartan collars, and at bedtime he would put them all to bed with a big kiss and a biscuit. I try to treat my children as well as he treated our three spaniels.

JEFFREY, AGE 37

Oh gosh, how didn't it [being a father]
change me? I became selfless, I knew what it was like
to be willing to give my life to someone—and I would,
hands down...I've never known that feeling before.

JOHN TRAVOLTA

There must always be a struggle between
a father and son, while one aims at power and
the other at independence.

SAMUEL JOHNSON

We thought he [my father] was a terror. We thought he
was this madman who wouldn't smile or anything. He was
painfully shy, he didn't know how to have a conversation.
That's probably why he was so brilliant onstage, because
suddenly he had dialogue to express himself. And the
more we as his children wanted his attention, the more
he withdrew....For Henry, his distance was his protection.

PETER FONDA

A man can't get rich if he
takes proper care of his family.

NAVAJO SAYING

Parents are the bones upon
which children sharpen their teeth.

PETER USTINOV

Having children makes you
no more a parent than
having a piano makes you a pianist.

MICHAEL LEVIN, *Lessons at the Halfway Point*

The little things make you a hero [to your children]. When you're there to help them pick out the perfect clothes for school and the perfect shoes. If you comb out the hair in the morning and if you help them with their breakfast—those are the kind of things, the little things, that make you a hero. Of course, needless to say, I become a double-hero if I invite them over to the studio when I'm filming and they can watch me film.

ARNOLD SCHWARZENEGGER

My family was musical. Everyone sang and played.
Only when I was a teenager did I discover that
everybody didn't do that.

LINDA RONSTADT

It was 1920 and I was about six years old. We went to Atlantic City in the summer for a big vacation. My dad, who did very wild things sometimes, saw an advertisement for a brand new and exciting adventure, a short flight over the Atlantic Ocean in a biplane, a very recent invention. Since there was only a seat for the pilot, my father sat on the struts for the 10-minute ride. My mother and I and my baby sister stood on the boardwalk in front of the Hotel Ritz and watched. I thought my father was the bravest man in the world.

MARJORIE, 85

It's a wise father that knows his own child.

WILLIAM SHAKESPEARE

My father turned my life around by
insisting I be more than I was and
by believing I could be more."

OPRAH WINFREY

Observe, my son, your father's bidding,
and reject not your mother's teaching;

PROVERBS 6:20-23

My father considered a walk
among the mountains as the
equivalent of churchgoing.

ALDOUS HUXLEY

When one has not had a good father,
one must create one.

FRIEDRICH NIETZCHE

Govern a family as you would
cook a small fish—very gently.

CHINESE PROVERB

It is easier to build strong children
than to repair broken men.

FREDERICK DOUGLASS

The man my brother knew as a
father was not the same one I'd
known. People change—even fathers.

LEO BUSCAGLIA

I talk and talk and talk, and I haven't taught people in fifty
years what my father taught me by example in one week.

MARIO CUOMO, *former governor of New York*

I don't mind looking into the mirror and seeing my father.

MICHAEL DOUGLAS

As a father of two
there is a respectful question
which I wish to ask of fathers of five:
How do you happen to be still alive?

OGDEN NASH

A good father is a little bit of a mother.

LEE SALK

The only fatherly advice I have ever
given...is to not eat your peas off a knife.

JOHN CHEEVER

The parent who leaves his son enormous wealth generally deadens the talents and energies of the son.

ANDREW CARNEGIE

My dad told me there's no difference between a black snake and a white snake. They both bite.

THURGOOD MARSHALL

A boy wants something very special from his father. You hear it said that fathers want their sons to be what they feel they cannot themselves be, but I tell you it also works the other way.

SHERWOOD ANDERSON

Every son, at one point or another, defies his father, fights him, departs from him, only to return to him—if he is lucky—closer and more secure than before.

LEONARD BERNSTEIN

Like any father, I have moments when I wonder whether I belong to my children or they belong to me.

BOB HOPE

My name is Nick.
My father thought of it shaving.

ABRAHAM & ZUCKER, *Top Secret*

My father's idea of dress-down Saturday was to wear a plaid viyella shirt with a plaid necktie. He didn't know how to hug me but he did the best with what he had, and I think that's very important.

ROBERT, AGE 63

Still as a dad, you have to be a father.
It's funny; sometimes it's almost like repossession.
I'm possessed by the spirit of my [late] father. "Don't do that!" All of a sudden, "Oh my God, it's my dad."

ROBIN WILLIAMS

A father is a banker provided by nature.

FRENCH PROVERB

In my younger and more vulnerable years my father gave me some advice that I've been turning over in my mind ever since.

"Whenever you feel like criticizing anyone," he told me, "just remember that all the people in this world haven't had the advantages that you've had."

F. SCOTT FITZGERALD, *The Great Gatsby*

My father is home, working in the cellar. I sit on the steps and watch. He asks why I don't go outside and play, but playing is dull beside the excitement of being with him. Times I am allowed to enter his world stand out like sentences highlighted in yellow.

DEBORAH TANNEN

Our relationship grew easier over the years. In time, it felt like friendship. Dad called me to discuss his poetry, what kind of car to buy and whether or not he should remarry. When together we sometimes sat quietly. There are few people in the world with whom I'm that comfortable.

RALPH KEYES, *author of The Wit & Wisdom of Harry Truman*

My poor daddy played my musical arrangements very badly. He wasn't much of a pianist, but he made my whole career as Baby Phyllis possible. He invented me, along with hypnotizing cats, hand-painted hat, and fortunetelling, so let's not look a gift daddy in the …well…at least not to closely…yet.

PHYLLIS NEWMAN, *actress*

Dads raised me to get outside, get muddy, and most of all—to get on with it... You want to get from A to B, you take the shortest path, the straight one, and you deal with any hurdles as they come.

SARAH, *Duchess of York*

Sometimes I see myself at my father's funeral. Gripping both sides of the lectern, I pause the way Dad would.... Then I launch into the one about the man who tells his wife he wants his ashes scattered in Bloomingdale's so he can be sure she'll come visit.

PATRICIA VOLK, *author of All It Takes*

This is Daddy's bedtime secret for today:
Man is born broken. He lives by mending.
The grace of God is glue.

EUGENE O'NEILL

A wise son makes his father glad,
but a foolish son is a grief to his mother.

PROVERBS 10:1

My dad…he'd try anything—carpentry, electrical wiring,
plumbing, roofing. From watching him, I learned a lesson
that still applies to my life today: No matter how difficult
a task may seem, if you're not afraid to try it…you can do
it. And when you're done, it will leak.

DAVE BARRY

I didn't know that fathers were not
supposed to hit kids if they were bad.
Most father hit kids—anybody's. The
kid whose father didn't hit him felt
that his father either wasn't interested
in him or wasn't his real father.

SAM LEVINSON *Everything But Money*

How did I know he was going to become
Leonard Bernstein? You know, every genius had
a handicap. Beethoven was deaf. Chopin had
tuberculosis. Well, someday I suppose the books
will say, "Lenny Bernstein had a father."

SAM BERNSTEIN, *remembering his opposition to his son's music career.*

A boy and his dad on a fishing trip—
Oh, I envy them, as I see them there
Under the sky in the open air,
For out of the old, old long ago
Come the summer days that I used to know,
When I learned life's truths from my father's lips
As I shared the joy of his fishing trips—
Builders of life's companionship.

EDGAR A. GUEST

"My fifteen-year-old son is talking about going away to prep
school.... "Now I'm losing my buddy. Who will watch the
Panthers win the Stanley Cup with me? Being a parent has
come to mean a great deal to me—and I don't want to lose
that."

INTERVIEW WITH GAIL SHEEHY, *Understanding Men's Passages.*

My father was not a failure. After all, he was
the father of a president of the United States.

HARRY TRUMAN

My dad can hit a home run, catch a big bluefish,
remember the whole Yankee World Series
statistics, and fix anything, but he never
can catch the 7:34 train.

ROBBIE, AGE 9

English history is all about men liking their fathers, and
American history is all about men hating their fathers and
trying to burn down everything they ever did.

MALCOLM BRADBURY

My father would come home and say, "You did well, but could you do better? It's hard out there." I would come home from school with a good grade, and my father would say, "Must have been an easy assignment…"

HILLARY RODHAM CLINTON

He [my father] would visit. We would row an old wooden boat on a twilight-still lake and … The two of us would regain the serenity I had felt when I was a child and he rowed us out onto the evening mirror of a small Adirondack lake. … I would tell him that he had taught me to find peace in the wilderness…and what had nagged between us would finally be still.

MARY SOJOURNER, *author of Sisters of the Dream*

I can run the country or
control Alice. I can't do both.

THEODORE ROOSEVELT

My father was … so absorbed in his own engineering work
that he seldom talked to us children at all, but he would
become communicative in the world of out-of-doors…I
treasured the nature walks Father and I took together.
Father could hide in the bushes and whistle bird calls so
convincingly that the birds he imitated came to him.

MARGARET BOURKE WHITE, *photographer*

Standing by the crib of one's own baby, with that world-old pang of compassion and protectiveness toward this so little creature…for the first time one understands the homely succession of sacrifices and pains by which life is transmitted and fostered down the stumbling generations of men.

CHRISTOPHER MORLEY

If the new American father feels bewildered and even defeated, let him take comfort from the fact that whatever he does in any fathering situation has a fifty percent chance of being right.

BILL COSBY, *Fatherhood*

Be kind to thy father, for when thou were young, Who loved thee as fondly as he? He caught the first accents that fell from thy tongue, And joined in thy innocent glee.

MARGARET COURTNEY, *19th century American poet*

He is an extraordinarily fine looking man.
He is the loveliest man I ever saw or hope to see.

SUSY CLEMENS, *about her father, Mark Twain*

To show a child what has once delighted you, to find the child's delight added to your own, so there is now a double delight seen in the flow of trust and affection, this is happiness.

J. B. PRIESTLEY, *author of Outcries and Asides*

If you live without being a father
you will die without being a human being.

RUSSIAN PROVERB

When I was 7 or 8 years old we moved to our own house in a new neighborhood. I felt miserable, left without friends. It was around this time that my father started a new family tradition. He always arrived with a surprise in one of his hands—a roll of LifeSavers! It made me feel special and loved. Years later, when Dad died, I slipped into the funeral home and put a roll of LifeSavers in his hands. "Thanks Dad, you are special and loved."

SANDI, 43

You are truly my son and not only
my son, but well-nigh the only happiness
and distraction that I have.

ALEXANDRE DUMAS

Sons have always a rebellious wish to be
disillusioned by that which charmed their fathers.

ALDOUS HUXLEY

...dad, who was the finest human being I have ever known, but who had the hairstyling skills and fashion flair of a lathe operator—cut my hair...This meant that I spent my critical junior high school years underneath what looked like the pelt of some very sick rodent.

DAVE BARRY

Blessed indeed is the man who hears
many gentle voices call him father!

LYDIA M. CHILD, *19th century writer*

None of you can ever be proud enough of being the child
of such a Father who has not his equal in the world—so
great, so good, so faultless. Try, all of you, to follow in his
footsteps and don't be discouraged, for to be really in
everything like him none of you, I am sure, will ever be.
Try, therefore, to be like him in some points, and you will
have acquired a great deal.

QUEEN VICTORIA *to the Prince of Wales, 1857*

His heritage to his children wasn't words or
possessions, but an unspoken treasure,
the treasure of his example as a man and a father.
More than anything I have, I'm trying to
pass that on to my children.

WILL ROGERS

I watched a small man with thick calluses on both hands
work fifteen and sixteen hours a day.... a man who came
here uneducated, alone, unable to speak the language,
who taught me all I needed to know about faith and hard
work by the simple eloquence of his example.

MARIO CUOMO, *former governor of New York*

What greater ornament to a son
than a father's glory, or to a father
than a son's honorable conduct?

SOPHOCLES

It doesn't matter who my father was;
it matters who I remember he was.

ANNE SEXTON, *Poet*

...any honest kid will tell you under oath, there are days
when kids can be quite impossible—like Monday
through Sunday. Come to think of it, the only perfect kid
I ever heard of was my father when he was a kid.

SAM LEVINSON, *Everything But Money*

I cannot think of any need in
childhood as strong as the
need for a father's protection.

SIGMUND FREUD

You appear to me so superior, so elevated above other
men. I contemplate you with such a strange mixture of
humility, admiration, reverence, love, and pride,
that very little superstition would be necessary to make
me worship you as a superior being.... I had rather not
live than not be the daughter of such a man.

THEODORA BURR, *to her father Aaron Burr*

I suppose that the high-water mark of my youth in Columbus, Ohio, was the night the bed fell on my father. It makes a better recitation ...than a piece of writing, for it is almost necessary to throw furniture around, shake doors, and bark like a dog, to lend the proper atmosphere and verisimilitude to what is admittedly a somewhat incredible tale. Still, it did take place.

JAMES THURBER, *My Life and Hard Times*

One father is more than a
hundred schoolmasters.

ENGLISH PROVERB

I wanted him to cherish and approve
of me, not as he had when I was a child,
but as the woman I was, who had her
own mind and had made her own choices.

ADRIENNE RICH, *poet*

It's clear that most American children
suffer too much mother and too little father.

GLORIA STEINEM

All three [children] have been, and continue to be, the joy
of my life, and of the many pieces of good fortune that
have been poured out on me I count this as the greatest.

KENNETH CLARK, *historian*

Manual labor to my father was not only good
and decent for its own sake, but as he was given to
saying, it straightened out one's thoughts.

MARY ELLEN CHASE, *author of A Goodly Heritage*

My son is here. I think that we do not know one another;
I think it is our destiny that we never will. I observe, in a
comical way, that he does not flush the toilet. He
observes that I snore. Another son returns tomorrow. I
feel that I know him better, but wait and see....Some part
of loving one's children is to part with them.

JOHN CHEEVER, *The Journals of John Cheever*

The debt of gratitude we owe our mother and father goes forward, not backward. What we owe our parents is the bill presented to us by our children.

NANCY FRIDAY, *author of My Mother, My Self*

Mr. Braddock: Don't you think that idea is a little half-baked?
Benjamin Braddock: Oh no, Dad, it's completely baked

CHARLES WEBB, *The Graduate*

What you have inherited from your father, you must earn over again for yourselves, or it will not be yours.

GOETHE

When a father, absent during the day,
returns home at six, his children receive
only his temperament, not his teaching.

ROBERT BLY, *author of Iron John*

One of my favorite things I love doing with my dad is
going fishing. We pack the cooler, and head down to the
boat. We go to our spot—we think it is the quietest spot
on the lake—and then we kick back, relax, take out our
fishing rods. We put on the radio and listen to some
Oldies, dad's favorites. I never liked fishing until I went
fishing with my dad. I don't know why, but fishing with
my dad is better than any day with my friends.

SEAN, AGE 15

To be a successful father there's one absolute rule:
when you have a kid, don't look at it for the first two years.

ERNEST HEMINGWAY

Father sticks to it that anything that promises
to pay too much can't help being risky.

DOROTHY CANFIELD FISHER, *author of Seasoned Timber*

It now costs more to amuse a child than
it once did to educate his father.

VAUGHAN MONROE, *comic*

The plan was to go to a summer camp together. Little Ruthie had been at this camp the year before and she described the sylvan, rugged beauty of that life to [my daughter] Barbara. Barbara said to Ruthie that she'd love to go but that she was afraid she would be lonesome, that she never had gone anywhere without her parents.

"Oh," said Ruthie, "after the third day you forget you ever had a father or mother.

LUDWIG BEMELMANS, *I Love You I Love You I Love You*

My father gave me these hints
on speech-making: "Be sincere…
be brief…be seated."

JAMES ROOSEVELT

I am indebted to my father for living,
but to my teacher for living well.

ALEXANDER THE GREAT

Education is something you get when
you father sends you to college. But it isn't
complete until you send your son there.

ANONYMOUS

It is admirable for a man to take his son fishing,
but there is a special place in heaven for the
father who takes his daughter shopping.

JOHN SINOR

It is a wise child that knows his own father.

HOMER

Fathers should be neither
seen nor heard. This is the only
proper basis for family life.

OSCAR WILDE

Father asked us what was God's noblest work.
Anna said men, but I said babies. Men after
all are often bad but babies never are.

LOUISA MAY ALCOTT

President Clinton…taking his child to college.
The most powerful man in the world admitted
his sense of utter powerlessness as a parent at
this stage. "There's nothing I can do now…
Nothing but what all parents finally have to
do: let go." The President comforted himself
by getting a dog.

GAIL SHEEHY *Understanding Men's Passages*

I felt something impossible for me to explain in words.
Then when they took her away, it hit me. I got scared
all over again and began to feel giddy. Then it came to
me—I was a father.

NAT KING COLE

When I was a boy of fourteen, my father
was so ignorant I could hardly stand to
have the old man around. But when I got
to be twenty-one, I was astonished at
how much he had learned.

MARK TWAIN

My father always wanted to be the corpse at
every funeral, the bride at every wedding and the
baby at every christening.

ALICE ROOSEVELT LONGWORTH, *daughter*
of President Theodore Roosevelt

The best money advice ever given me was from
my father. When I was a little girl, he told me,
"Don't spend anything unless you have to."

DINAH   SHORE

When I was very little and didn't have
any money, I would make a booklet of
coupons for my father to buy special
chores from me. For $5.00 he could
have two leaf rakings, one back massage,
or one afternoon when I would clean
my room. He loved it!

REEVE, AGE 12

It is impossible to please all
the world and also one's father.

LA FONTAINE

Papa believed the greatest sin of which we were capable
was to go to bed at night as ignorant as we had been
when we wakened that day.

LEO BUSCAGLIA

Raising teenagers: The first rule is roll with the punches.
The second rule is roll with the punches. And the third
rule is roll with the punches. You're going to get punchy,
but keep doing it.

ROBERT FULGHUM, *author of*
All I Really Need to Know I Learned in Kindergarten

The impression the father makes on his son's friends...
is important enough to leave eradicable scars. Take the
time the kid is playing in the street with his friends, and
let one of the other kids say, *"Johnny , here comes your
father."* Now you have one of the most important
moments in a boy's life. Do you have any idea what
goes through his mind during that fleeting moment?
Your appearance, your dress, your walk, your manner,
what you say to your son in greeting, and what you say
to the other kids; these are matters of life and death to
the son, whose heart thumps wildly through the ordeal.
Of course, this is something he will never discuss with
you. You'll never find out from him. You must discover
it yourself.

HARRY GOLDEN, *Only in America*

Oh, it's nice [becoming a father again].
It's exciting, it's a rich experience.
There's the dream you have and the
expectations for a newborn. There's
much more patience in my being,
and a sense of wonderment of life
and how precious it is.

PIERCE BROSNAN

I remember daddy's hands how they held my mama tight
And patted my back for something done right
There are things that I'd forgotten that I loved about the man
But I'll always remember the love in daddy's hands.

HOLLY DUNN, *Country music singer*

Life doesn't come with
an Instruction Book
that's why we have fathers.

H. JACKSON BROWN, *Life's Little Instruction Book*

... Daddy was out in back working on his lawn—leveling and seeding it, whistling as he wheelbarrowed dirt from one end of our lot to the other. He was proud of the fact that we had twice a much yard as any of our neighbors. He worked every night until dark—until he faded from himself to a dusky silhouette, then a glowing white undershirt ...

WALLY LAMB, *She's Come Undone*

"Twenty-five years ago," the woman
said, "we made a promise to one
another. I would never have to clean
a fish, and he would never have
to know if his daughter was pregnant."

ANNA QUINDLEN, *Thinking Out Loud*

Close your eyes,
Have no fear,
The monster's gone,
He's on the run and your daddy's here...

JOHN LENNON

Wonderful little our fathers knew
Half their remedies cured you dead—
Most of their teaching was quite untrue.

RUDYARD KIPLING

Mother says that Father spends too much time with his
horse friends....Mother will not go to any horse shows
with him, so I get to take her place. I love all the ladies in
the jodhpurs and boots, and the picnics with vodka gim-
lets for the grown-ups and pink lemonade for me...

REBECCA WELLS, *Divine Secrets of the Ya-Ya Sisterhood*

When his children were young he would take them ... to the park around five in the morning...It was then that the retirees from the local opera company gathered to vocalize... All five of his children had learned how to perform. Whatever the singers did, he'd had the children do. When they sang an aria, his children sang an aria; when they danced, his children danced; when they mimed, his children mimed...Aping professionals...was an efficient way to learn; and what's more, the lessons were free.

BETTY BAO LORD, *Legacies: A Chinese Mosaic*

When the good Lord was creating fathers
He started with a tall frame.

And a female angel nearby said, "What
kind of father is that? If You're going to make
children so close to the ground, why have
You put fathers up so high? He won't be able
to shoot marbles without kneeling, tuck a
child in bed without bending, or even kiss
a child without a lot of stooping."
And God smiled and said, "Yes, but if I
make him child-size, whom would children
have to look up to?"

ERMA BOMBECK

When Rabbi Joseph hear his mother's footsteps he would say, "I will rise before the approaching [Divine Presence].

BABYLONIAN TALMUD

Michael Corleone: My father is no different than any powerful man, any man with power, like a president or senator.
Kay Adams: Do you know how naive you sound, Michael? Presidents and senators don't have men killed!
Michael Corleone: Oh. Who's being naive, Kay?

FRANCIS FORD COPPOLA, *The Godfather*

"Papa, I've been writing a book."

"Have you , my dear?"

"Yes, and I want you to read it."

"I am afraid it will try my eyes too much."

"But it is not in manuscript; it is printed."

"My dear! you've never thought of the expense it will be! It will be almost sure to be a loss, for how can you get a book sold?..."

So she sat down and read some of the reviews to her father; and then, giving him a copy of *Jane Eyre* that she intended for him, she left him to read it. When he came in to tea, he said, "Girls, do you know Charlotte has been writing a book, and it much better than likely?"

Conversation between CHARLOTTE BRONTE AND HER FATHER

A father is always making his baby
into a little woman. And when she is
a woman he turns her back again.

ENID BAGNOLD, *English novelist*

I have found the best way to give
advice to your children is to find out what
they want and then advise them to do it.

HARRY S. TRUMAN

My father was a statesman,
I'm a political woman.
My father was a saint. I'm not.

INDIRA GANDHI

A man must not dishonor his father in his speech. How so? For example if the father is old and wants to eat early in the morning, as old men do, and he asks his son for food, and the son says, "The sun has not yet risen, and you're already up and eating!"...

ISRAEL BEN JOSEPH AL-NAKAWA, *14th century scholar*

Mr. Strickland: You don't have a chance, you're too much like your old man. No McFly ever amounted to anything in the history of Hill Valley!
Marty McFly: Yea, well, history is gonna change.

ROBERT ZEMECHIS & BOB GALE, *Back to the Future*